VIRAHA

Poems by

Yena Sharma Purmasir

VIRAHA

ISBN: 979-8-9858207-6-8

Cover design and layout Sam Cush.

Edited by Aly Pierce and Josh Savory.

www.gameoverbooks.com

"Sometimes I think I'm never going to write a poem again
and then there's a full moon.

I miss being in love but I miss
myself most when I'm gone."

—Camonghne Felix, "Born. Living. Will Die." (2021)

SUMMER NIGHT

When the summer sun sets, I can leave my cage
without the stench of sunscreen. I hate everything
I have learned to fear: men, cancer, my own mortality.
One day when I'm not beautiful and no one loves me,
I hope I can go up to the mountains. I hope I can go
to the beach. I hope the trees in my hometown remember
me as more than a girl. I used to eat ice cream in the park.
I used to bike down the boulevard. I used to fall on my knees
and cry like I invented crying. I wish I invented something.
Is it too late? I waited for my life and the bus drove on.
The whole sky changed.

LINGUISTICS

Words should sound like what they mean. *Harm*
sounds warm. I hold a bad thought like I hold
a lover. I wear it like a locket. *Locket* sounds like
a secret. I tell no one.

I disappear twice a week. I come back.
Back is an animal noise. I'm a girl.
I'm still waiting to grow up. *Up* is a hiccup.
Still is a lake I can't swim.

BUZZ

We ate sushi when we were supposed to eat arepas.
Nothing turned out the way I thought it would: you
were no one & then you were someone; you were kind
& then you were cold; you were there & then you were
drunk. Another beer for my friend who isn't my friend,
who lost his sponsor / scholarship / life.
I would pour the coffee back in the pot, unclean
my bed, never check my email if it would undo
your shaking hands.

No, I take that back. I don't care about
your shaking hands
        midnight grief
                little problems.

Here are my problems, that you never let me hold,
that were only relevant because they made me
interesting. My pain like a lighthouse.

This is an elegy for my once upon a time joy.

SPINSTER

LAST YEAR TWO MEN TOLD ME THEY WOULDN'T MARRY ME / TWO MEN I LOVED / I LOVED TWO MEN / I LOVED TOO MANY MEN / & THIS ISN'T THE KINDEST MOMENT TO REMEMBER / I WANT TO IMMEDIATELY OFFER UP THE MEMORY OF / CHRISTMAS APPLE PIE / FRESH OCTOBER CIDER / TO PROVE IT WASN'T ALL / UNNECESSARY CRUELTY / BUT THE MEN I LOVED / WHO THREW THEIR CONTACT LENSES & CONDOM WRAPPERS RIGHT ON THE FLOOR / THEIR GARBAGE BECAME MY GARBAGE / THAT I HAD TO SHIFT THROUGH / & WHAT IS LOVE IF NOT A TRANSFORMATION? / I WAS A PERSON UNTIL I HAD A FEELING / AWAKE IN BED & GRATEFUL FOR THE SNORING BODY / THAT NEVER BECAME MORE THAN A BODY / NO MATTER ALL MY BLINKING / I'M STILL SEEING WHEN I SHOULD BE SLEEPING / IF I GET TO BE A WIFE / I PROMISE MY MIND WILL DRIFT / LET SOMEONE ELSE KEEP VIGIL / I AM TIRED OF MY COMPASS-JUMP HEART / I WANT TO SETTLE DOWN / I AM SEARCHING FOR THE NORTH STAR / THE NORTH START THAT KEEPS MOVING / I KEEP MOVING / IS THAT NOT WHAT WIVES DO? / I WOULDN'T KNOW / I'VE NEVER HAD A WIFE / WHEN I NEEDED TO BE A PERSON / I WASHED MY FACE / I MADE MY BED / I MOURNED THE DEAD THING LIKE I LOVED / THE DEAD THING / I LOVED THE DEAD THING LIKE A WIDOW / I WAS A WINDOW LEFT OPEN / A GLASS PANE IN PAIN / A WHOLE WORLD BEHIND ME / THE UNMARRIED SUN ON ME

DEATH CARD

When is it permissible to kill?

Never

What if she hurt me?

Irrelevant

What if she meant to?

Impossible

What if she wasn't like us?

Everyone is like us

What if it happened this way, what
if she looked like you & wasn't you, what
if she attacked like a lion & wasn't a lion, what
if she made me want to die & when I didn't die,
all that was left was the range of my rage,
my pained song, my worst act, lurking like
a shadow   *It isn't a shadow*
following me like a promise?   *It isn't a promise*
What if you loved me   *I love you*
& there was an evil   *I don't believe in evil*
face up on the table?   *Leave the table*
You want me to suffer   *I want you to change*
like a hanged man   *like a fool*
with my head in hell.   *with your chest opened*

PROTECTION SPELL

You are a sailor. I am the moon.
My best thoughts are following you
home. You round the corner of the world
and there, against belief, is the tide
of peace. O may no one ever hurt you;
may no one ever want to. In my clearest
dreams, you move through a mustard field
and the bees let you. Real love is yellow.
You blend in like a star. I told God about you
like God isn't in charge. In my strangest
dreams, I'm in charge and the universe echoes
my sky. My religion has exactly two rules:
there is always someone like me praying for
someone like you; there is always someone
like you.

CAVEWOMAN

There is a cave inside me. I lived there
for years. A man drove me to it. I feared
his hand inside me & I wanted a hand
inside me, to be a puppet girl made real.

You don't have to blame me, I blamed me.
You don't have to forgive me, I forgave me.

My cave was good to me. I should be good
to my cave, the sacred place that held me
when I wouldn't let anyone else hold me.

But I resent my cave, the dark lonely space
that ate into me. My cave became me.

And it didn't matter how kind someone else
was, how gentle, how patient. When he touched
me, how I trembled, how I came tumbling down.

MOON TIME

You thought I was wet, when I was just bloody:
stood up too quickly & out leaked the mess of me.
I want to have a baby, if a baby will have me. Until
then, I'll keep loving men in need of mothering,
nurse their idiot ideas, cradle their dwindling
self esteem, clean up their shit, put them to bed.
The last time I had sex might be the last time
I have sex, I'm still deciding. It's not that I regret
the snoring mouth in my ear. It's the memory
of his slouching body stretched out in the morning.
It doesn't fit our nothing story. Who cares about
his soft belly, floppy hair, medium roast laugh?
Every man is the same man. Every baby has the
same stupid slobber smile. Every mother thinks she's
so different: her big fucking heart, the size of the sun.
(And then she has a son.)

RED CARDINAL

There is a world in which I die.
You don't. My best friend, you live forever. You go
alone to the places we said we would explore together.
In Vietnam, you buy an expensive camera. You take
pictures of your face the way I took pictures of my face.
You hate the vacant expressions on my Instagram. No one
ever knew me there. I can't point out the glittering silver
lining from beyond the grave. Honey, I don't have a grave.
When you want to visit me, you'll have to collect a bouquet
of superstitions: an out-of-focus dream, the pink supermoon,
a red cardinal on your windowsill. This terrible world loves you
like I have loved you, which means you know it
and you think it happens to everyone.
(It does not happen to everyone.)

MYTH #1

At first, there was everything.
You sang our forever song.
I didn't know how to cry & had no reason to learn.

Then there was a reason. Then another. It built
like an empire. I died like a fire. I was a fire
& you were the wind. You were the wind &
I hurt. There was a war I waged &

it doesn't matter who won. It ended.
The war. The sun. The dipper in the sky tipped
over. I stole the river from the ocean.

I cried like a mother. (*I had no mother.*)
I cried like a daughter. (*I had no daughter.*)
Love changed me. I became a planet.

I was alone.

THINGS THAT AREN'T TRUE

after Mayra Morales

My father was right-handed. My mother left.
My brother was not born in a hospital.
My father did not die in a hospital.

I grew up in a small town with one long road.
I love cars. I learned how to drive before my first period.
The first time a boy kissed me, my feet were on the ground.
The first time I kissed a boy, his feet were on the ground.
I was a child. It was not perfect. He was not perfect.
The last time I saw him, I felt nothing. I didn't love him,
which isn't my fault. It's the way of the forest.

It's an old story. The women in my family leave first.
I've got my mother's face and her mother's hair.
They kept my baby hair. I was a bird until I was a girl.
Bless the animal who raised me.

DOPPELGÄNGER

"The ethical function of the appearance of the double is obviously the same as the ethical function of death, i.e., the loss of existence of the subject. Or shall we say that the loss of concreteness brings about a depersonalization of the subject: it becomes a 'thing,' it loses existence as a subject. Thus the double puts with extreme power the question: will the individual discover a new stability and a new life in absolute being or will he perish in Nothingness?"

—Dmitri Chizhevksy, *The Theme of the Double in Dostoyevsky*

My favorite actor was never supposed to be my husband.
He was the shadow of my father. Shah Rukh Khan dancing badly
and confidently. My father in a wheelchair,
asking me why I even liked him.

I don't know, I said. *I cry when I look at him*, I said.

When I was a child, I would rewind and repeat my favorite scenes,
watching his weepy brown eyes, seeing his dimples reveal
and hide.

When *Kuch Kuch Hota Hai* was released, my father couldn't come
with us to the cinema. My father hardly ever came with us to the cinema.
I watched the movie and sobbed through the entire second half.

At home, he asked my mother why I was so upset. *You can't
see these movies anymore*, he said, because he was worried.
I was six years old and bawling.

I'm not sad, I said. *It's just love*, I said.

Life is so hard, I said.

When my father died, he really died. There is no way to see him again.
But I have watched every Shah Rukh Khan movie, just in case.
And if his hair is gray, if he is limping, if he is smoking
or shaking,

it is almost the same.

Once, I had a dream I met Shah Rukh Khan.
We were in the middle of the street. He was getting out of a car.
I ran up to him and said in broken Hindi:

Aap mujhe jaante nahin, lekin aap mere pita ki yaad dilaatee hai.
>   [English subtitles: You don't know me, but you
>   remind me of my father.]

Kya main aapko gale laga sakati hoon?
>   [English subtitles: Can I hug you?]

Kya main aapko choo sakati hoon?
>   [English subtitles: Can I touch you?]

Shah Rukh Khan smiled at me and let me put my head on his chest.
Pagli, he said, *maine tujhe pehchana.*
>   [English subtitles: Silly girl, I recognize you.]

I see you everywhere.

GROWING PAINS

pinned like a butterfly, plucked like an upper lip,
girlhood has prepared me for a lifetime of motion sickness:

hovering over a toilet seat, blotting my lipstick
and blowing my nose with the same tissue.

the worst thing that has happened to my body
is my disappointment.

there is no pain like a lover abandoning you
and i am waving goodbye to the things i don't like
in the mirror, on facebook, in this poem

that is not exactly a poem, because no one is crying,
because no one is afraid that i'm dying. no one is praying
or saying my name, which is a relief:

no one says my name like i say my name.

THE SECOND MOUNTAIN

The year after my first summer at camp was the summer
immediately following Miley Cyrus's release of "The Climb"

This was back when Hannah Montana was still alive
back when I was sixteen & in Denmark,
where the word for *mountain* & *hill* are the same

& hiking meant watching one teenager fumble with a compass
& another with the laminated map

Before we went off course,
I got a tick bite on my neck that Ilze tried to remove
with tweezers in a national park

but she couldn't get the head,
not even when Clay held a flashlight
like a halo over me & the persistent July sun

No later after we ate three dinners of rice & cheese
& carried our packs over our heads through a stream
the size of my confidence,
I had to sit in the infirmary stinking of tea tree oil

Ilze dug into my skin with a needle & a younger me
would have cried at the invasion or the thought of Lyme disease
but I was a veteran, a leader, a girl
with a passport

& I was done flinching

I called my mom only because I was told to
& she said, *Don't they have hospitals in this country*
& I said, laughing because the distance between us
made everything ridiculous, *Ma it looks like a hickey*

The summer before, the girls in the next tent
gave each other hickies
for practice or pleasure or the pain of it all,
which if you remember being fifteen, you know was grandiose

That was an American camp on American soil
& it was the Danish girl who bruised the pinkest,
the girl from Jersey who laughed so loud
even us New Yorkers were envious

I can almost see that farmhouse but the rest of the song
is out of reach

If I think too hard, Hannah stops crooning

I learned a lesson in girlhood that summer
that doesn't make sense out of the wilderness

No one could believe what we did to survive
how the least adventurous of us could bring down an axe
like a fucking thunderclap

& given the day, we cried together like a monsoon

In English, is there a word for a group of girls crying?
Is that word *stop*?

VIRAHA (विरह)

Steve told me that half the pleasure in love was being half
of something, separated and praying for reunion.
It's not just us, he said, *it's the gods.*

I love this story. I love how small it makes my pain.

I tell the man I'm dating, we're just like gods,
but that doesn't have the same humility.
It sounds like I'm boasting.

Okay, so I'm boasting. Someone loves me finally
and I'm cutting my hair over the toilet.
Someone loves me finally and my waist is shrinking down.

I mean, my mental illness isn't going away
but it isn't really hanging around either.

When I say I'm lonely, what I really mean
is that I miss someone. When I say I miss someone,
what I really mean is you.

A GOOD PLACE

I.
I was taught a lesson in object permanence
decades before my time, by my immigrant parents,
who had seen whole countries shift. Nothing lasts
forever, not home or the manger He was born in.

This is a good thing. This is a good place,
though I may never come here again. Though
the land might give and pipes might burst,

though no other child may know this river.
I admit even I do not know this river.

II.
When you're not from somewhere, you eat its history
with greedy fists, hoping to become
and belong.

If you keep going like this, one day you might
decide that you too want to own, want to put
your name on something that already has a name.

You don't know it, so you don't learn it, so
you don't teach it.

III.
I hate stories about property because they're boring.
I only like the parts when people give up,
like my parents who gave up everything

to come to this country, where their daughter
could go to a camp that holds onto old newspapers
and photographs, so nothing is forgotten.

I like the endings, how it feels to walk out of a room
that no one else will walk into, how open the sky is
and how no one fears it.

IV.
This was a good place and then someone sang
about destiny and God. No one mentions God
until God is supposed to decide something.

The last time I was in the sacred house
that men who have outlived my father fiercely love,
the ceiling tiles started to fall.

You know how big the world is. To think
that God is here right now, watching in silence
doesn't make sense.

Forget the clatter and the hiccupping frogs,
God is speaking. God has a theory and name.
I have a name. Call me—

damsel; WOMAN

when the man i loved tried to save me, he sat
across from me at the dining table, refused to let me
talk until i made half my sandwich disappear and then,
the other half.

was proud of my hips, was seduced by my waist,
liked my body and wanted me to like my body.

got serious when i joked about a no chocolate diet,
got out of bed. came back with nutella, peanut butter,
a six pack of ramen noodles that i didn't have to slurp alone.

made a ring with his fingers, a bangle on my wrist.
my baby grown up wrist, can be snapped under
the weight of a different life, can be shaped
into a different position.

he said he didn't want me to die and my white dress
slipped from my shoulders.

once he took me in front of a mirror
to show me how small i was, how i could never
quite measure up, and i almost liked it.

once he rubbed his leg against mine
and everything he could be, he offered to me,
serving size be damned and it happened.

i became big. i stretched like a universe, i filled like a cup,
i spilled over like a waterfall and i gathered like a lake.

and have you ever heard of a lake disappearing?
ever imagined the devastation suffered by a colossal thing?
ever laughed at the thought of drowning in a spoonful of water?

ever diminished to punish? ever stopped to love?

HIGHS & LOWS

He said he smoked, but he just meant at the party once
and even then, his brother drove him home. When he first
told me this, we were zipping through the city in his dad's car.
But the confession was in his room, sitting on a beanbag chair.
When someone tells me he is drinking again in bars, I think of
the sober driver, smiling at me over a glass of water. I'm not
straight edge, but I'm scared. I hate when my brother lights up
and I hate the stories he tells us after. Liz's mom told me
to never marry a man who does drugs. It's old lady advice but
I know what she means. It's scary when men are in control
and scarier when they are not. My father when he lost it
threw chocolate cake against the walls. The man I loved
told me he just wanted to be good and then after I left,
he still was. It doesn't make you bad, baby, just different.
Now, he rides down to the beach, stoned and hungry.
When he texts me back, he writes in jumbled sentences,
says he's sorry, says that's probably the wrong thing.

SUMMER TAN

We were saying goodbye
and all I could think about was time and eyelashes;

if I had all the time in the world with you,
I would still be amazed at the length of your eyelashes

but since time was not enough,
I thought instead of the wishes you could blink into existence.

My evergreen sweetheart,
I see in you the gentle slope of a mountain,
imagine kissing you with the same reverence as loving you.

You are all curve and muscle, hunger growing into body,
my hands lingering on calf and shoulder, touching,
resting.

My summer evening in a bottle. Your wet hair in the morning.

Our feet nestled underneath a picnic table,
undressing as mosquitos fed from our naked abundance
and trying not to scratch, or laugh.

None of this can be done again. We are not here anymore.
I am sewing together a hammock and you are drinking apple cider.

What you loved about me should be fading like a summer tan,
but I'm brown. I'm brown forever.

THE RETELLING

first there was a fire test; Rama was not an unreasonable man
but he was a king
Sita had been away for so long and it made sense

he told her, it just made sense

when I was younger, I didn't know the word for rape,
just the scary bits in movies, of women saying no
and men looming closer, closer

what happened then, no one knew

there is a big point in this story:
Ravana never touched Sita.

there is a big point in this story: Rama knows
Ravana never touched Sita.

Esmeralda is a not a Disney princess
in a movie for children and she is called, over and over again,
by a slur

Frollo wants the Romani people to die and pleads with God for it,
a white God
a God who has heard these pleas before

Rama is an incarnate of Vishnu
and he is supposed to be good

when Valmiki tells this story, he tries hard, so hard
to keep Rama good

in their origin story, the Romani people say India
the Romani people can say any truth they want

no one is listening

Frollo doesn't want Esmeralda to dance
because he doesn't want her to stop

Sita walked through the fire and survived,
turning flames to flowers

which should have been the first lesson
but the magic seemed safe

Rama thought he was finally safe

but it doesn't end like this, Esmeralda on the stake
in a white dress

it is important that the girl is always in a white dress

Frollo saying she will burn in hell for this sin
or the next

Esmeralda's body has never burned for anything

when I was a child, I wanted to be her, dark skin
and long skirts

the way my mother dresses for temple

at temple, if your waist peeks out from the folds of your sari
there is a lady who will pinch you

in God's house there are rules,
she says

Esmeralda doesn't have a fire test,
she has a near death experience

and then there is one man saving her

throwing her over to someone else

how come Esmeralda has to find love?
why can't she just take her hooped earrings and dance
away from France?

Sita passed the fire test, so I never understand this part
Rama loved her, so I never understand this part

but there was another test and this time
she got angry

have you ever seen a goddess get angry?

this whole time, did you forget she was a goddess?

we're not dealing with a capitalist retelling here,
Sita called her mother

have you ever seen a daughter call her mother,
ever heard her say

can you come get me? I want to go home

ever watched a goddess slip back inside the earth

ever seen a god-man sorry

does it matter that Rama was sorry
that he had a golden Sita statue by his side

that Valmiki promised, imagine a storyteller promising,
that there would be other lives

in another life, Sita doesn't get hurt

in another life, Esmeralda can get married and stop
dancing on the street

but Esmeralda loves dancing on the street,
tells everyone she can't stay anywhere for long,
tells everyone she wants to be out

but who cares, she's in a white dress,

always put the girl in a white dress,
always wipe off her makeup and tell her that love can save her

have you ever seen love save a woman?

why are the credits rolling? I want to see
what happens when Esmeralda marries a soldier

I want to see what happens when they go home

do you think Rama ever hit Sita?
am I the only girl who ever wondered that?

right, Ravana never touched Sita,
Ravana never touched Sita

but Rama? Rama her husband
Rama is a god, right

God doesn't listen to those pleas, right

look, no one is supposed to think that
Sita and Esmeralda are the same

not all brown people are the same

just because it looks like the same Halloween costume
doesn't mean it is the same Halloween costume

anyway, the monsters have come out of hiding
and we're praying to them

anyway, there is a word for rape
and a word for a fire test
and a word that cuts down a people dispersed

having a language has made us unreasonable,
none of these things should make sense

but everyone knows,
you know what I'm talking about

ALPHABET SONG FOR THE 21ST CENTURY

A is for anonymous, because this isn't just me.
B is for beauty, which no longer matters.
C is for citizenship and how to renounce it.
D is for depth, but you're floating.
E is for earth, but she's dying.
F is for factories and the skyline changing.
G is for gun control, which no one believes in.
H is for heaven, that doesn't exist.
I is for illegal, but the rules can change.
J is for journal, but who wants to remember?
K is kerosene and the funeral pyres.
L is for listening to the radio.
M is for music on the radio.
N is for news on the radio.
O is for the off button on the radio.
P is for police and not calling them.
Q is for quiet, which is missed when it isn't.
R is for resistance and the river that demands it.
S is for someday, which we might never see.
T is for tonight, which needs a vigil and a hashtag.
U is for universe, that began with a bang and exists in a whimper.
V is for vintage, or the cost of keeping the past present.
W is for the wagon and all the people stepping off.
X is for xanax and the diagnosis to get it.
Y is for yearning, because there is never enough.
Z is for zodiac, but the sky is falling and the circle is broken.

BUBBLEGUM POP

I rode my bike under the blooming moon,
everything was bigger than me:

the trees,
the sky,
the men on the corner who followed me
home and asked for my name.

My name was bigger than me,
all those letters tangled the alphabet.

I had no alphabet. I gave up on words.
I held on to laughter. I boomed like thunder.

A little girl with a little pink bike.
My smile ate up my face.

WARDEN

for k

first an apology, no an addendum: it was
the worst time in my young life when you,
hair like a cornfield, sauntered into a room
& i girl with no heart only gaping chest wanted
to feel a tiny piece of joy. the dark trees bent under
the strain of your heavy gaze. our fingers barely touched.
i loved the way you searched the ground for my missing
ring until you found it & when you found it, how you let
me slip it back on myself. k, we never got married &
anyway i didn't want that with you or anyone who
wasn't half ghost, but if i was ever the sleep
on your pillow, i hope that dream woman let you
show her your mother's garden, that bloomed
& billowed every august under a specific sun.
i barely remember your slice of the constellation
to recheck our compatibility, but if i did i'm sure
it would say that you should run; you should run far
away & i like any almost-good thing would not follow.

EMAIL SETTINGS

subject: I AM OUT OF CONTROL,
re: too dramatic, so I drink some water and practice
my squats in dressing rooms

bcc: no one who loves me is touching me
me included, me in closets, purging everything

that isn't bringing me joy, but file://I AM NOT BRINGING ME JOY
and it's a shame. what made me special has also made me
cruel,

re: dangerous,

re: hurting. me tornado girl,
thinking all spinning is revolutionary

me, tornado
not girl, signature twisting,
signature laughing

REFRACTION

The way you knew me is unlike the way anyone else knows me.

The person I have always wanted to be is the person I am.

In the very beginning of our love, I had said one of us
is a small town hazard.

I am living in a city big enough for everyone's nightmares,
My heart is not just a ticking time bomb,
it's a clock unwinding. It's the sound on your nightstand.

When we first started drawing maps, we were so careful
with the scale. Somewhere in this mess, I think I drew
my own heart too big. I am never going to stretch myself again.

By the time you read this, it won't be quite as sincere. I love
the way you do laundry. If you can wash love out, I hope
it has already happened.

Do you think some people can see us for who we are?
What happens when they look away?

MYTH #2

I died. All the lights turned off. You
became the darkness. The moon went home.
Mercury spun until there was no way to walk off
its retrograde.

I faded like a star. I vanished like a love.
I was gone and the universe carried on.

One day, in some other world, an astronaut
will give up her time / space / life for a flicker
of my old light.

To her, I say: *don't.*

FIBONACCI SEQUENCE

I want to line up all the men I've loved in a row:
look them in the eye, each one more like my father
than the world ever let me be; measure their shoulders
against my shoulders; ask them to fill the tiniest space
in their crevice hearts for me; smell their nightmare
morning breath; tell them I see their perfect faces
on the passersby, always smiling / frowning / slack-jawed;
trade in my forgiveness for their friendship; promise them
I'll be okay.

SPRINTER

The past thinks it knows me. I used to be
that person. My skeleton was good:
a house with just enough natural light.
There was an old soulmate who kissed me
like no one ever kissed me. There was a time
when no one kissed me. I was the unburied
princess. Love saved me. Now into the future
I run. I can't see that far ahead but I promised
I'd be there. The bridge of my heart is waiting
for me to cross the world behind me:
      don't turn around / miss / long
      there is more to life than love

DRAFTED

Instead of writing that letter, I am writing this poem.
This is a draft. I'll come back and make it perfect.
I have forever. The sun tomorrow is supposed
to loom over the city like a Christmas angel.
I love Christmas. I'm already dreaming of what
I'll write in the greeting cards: how there were dark days /
long phone calls / a moon phase that hurt me /
a moon phase that healed me. I write best in the past tense.
I hate the present. I love the future. I am running away
from myself. If I'm ever someone else, I know I'll miss
the underbelly of the person who disbelieved love.
That person can do anything.

ALTERNATE METHODS OF DATING

after Lyd Havens

Think their name so often it becomes a feeling. Punctuate
your stream of consciousness texts with links to covers
of "Don't Stop Believin'." Tell your best friend you're
"in love" and tell your mom "it's not serious." Confess you
rewatch their stories via DM, but leave out the winking emoji.
Stop using emojis altogether. Draw a picture of your
smiling face that is all teeth and send it to their work email.
It doesn't matter how they respond, just that each notification
forever rewires your old desktop heart. Make plans that aren't
even plans. Talk about countries like seasons and seasons
like time isn't everything. Kiss them goodbye with all
the passion and grief reserved for someone you might
never see again. When you see them again, say their name
like it's nothing.

ECHELON

you said, & i barely remember the context, just that i admitted
that i had no idea what it meant. (an arrangement of a
body —) we were sitting at the terminal waiting to board
a plane so tiny it felt like a toy. you were just a boy
& there was nothing but your rescued wallet between us,
a plane ticket that i used in someone else's name, the airport
security agent who laughed when i set off the alarm. obviously,
this is a story from a different time, in a different place. obviously
i was the hero, the girl, the bird (— a flight formation), until you said
a word i had never heard before. even now, when i see it in the newspaper,
i think of you, that trip, the world's favorite ocean beneath us
the first thing you taught me.

MILKY WAY

You have turned my world, my atlas man.
I would go to another continent just
to dream of you during the in-flight movie.

You are the sweetest part of my candy bar
life. You make me want to eat a truffle.
You make me want to live forever.

I wish for more time in the melody
of your guitar solo. I would lipstick-kiss you
all over your asymmetrical face.
I would give up lipstick.

You would hate it. You, holding up
everything, would never ask me
to give up anything.

YELLOW

A perfect morning, there is such a thing.
Unslept, half a dream:

you lean your whole body into mine;
we melt like emerald green

      (your daffodil mouth)
      (my sapphire heart)

Somewhere the color red is shaking.
You are my primary. I close my eyes
& there, in the dark, is a bright warm
something. You break open my sky.

SHLOKA IN BIRDSONG

There are two birds on a branch
and one eats its heart out

because it can,
because the heart tastes good,

like pulp. Not everyone
likes pulp.

The other bird watches.
The other bird is never hungry.
The other bird wants for nothing.

There are two birds on a branch
and you would think the branch
has no story. This is the song of

two birds

always together on the same tree,
don't worry about the tree.

There are two birds and the love
between them is nothing like
the pattering of a hummingbird's heart;

it is the endless noise of quiet
that slowly seeps its way into everything.

There are two birds on a branch
and in one version they fly,

their perfect bodies like an arrow
in the sky.

There is one arrow in the sky and there
are two birds and then

there is one bird.

The other bird is gone. The other bird
with its beautiful red body, has more red
than body.

One bird cries and it breaks the mellow
of the riverside. One bird without her mate,

an incomplete pairing, a metaphor with
no reference to a real thing.

One bird and you want to look away,
to find the arrow's hand and curse the man,
who is like any man.

This is not about a man. There is one bird
and she screams into the abyss of solitude
for the injustice of all things.

She is one bird and we will never know
which bird:

if she ate the fruit of life
while her lover looked on,

or if she looked on while her lover,
stunning and indulgent, bit into
the most fleeting ripeness.

It doesn't matter. There are two birds,
there is one bird,
a branch,
a tree,
a river,
you, me.

We sit together in my open heart
that overflows with birdsong.
I am your sweetest thing.

And you, my companion through the universe,
I see the glory of your crest everywhere.

When you are gone, there will still be hills
and mountains and waves. When I am gone,

you will eat your heart out

because you can,
because the heart, loved and loving,
tastes good.

NEW MOON

THE BIRD INSIDE MY CHEST IS SCREAMING AT ME
TO RECOGNIZE THE BEAUTY OF THIS MOMENT BEFORE
IT IS GONE

AND WHILE IT IS STILL HERE, I WANT TO PROMISE
NOT TO RUN
NOT TO WORRY
NOT TO PRAY

THERE IS NOTHING TO SAY
EXCEPT TO OFFER THANKS

EXCEPT TO HOLD LIFE CLOSE
AND THINK NOT OF THE NEXT MOMENT
WHEN IT MIGHT SLIP AWAY

PERHAPS IT WON'T

A BOAT; A FISH

When Earth exploded, the bed ricocheted and the vase
of flowers spilled. Your mother gave me that vase but the flowers,
I had picked myself. I would have called you but my phone never had
service or courage again. The fault line of our country began
under my doorstep. Every time we kissed on the porch,
Rūaumoko[1] would laugh. He waited to pull the ropes to my backyard
until we were hundreds of kilometers away. Can you imagine
being married to the goddess of the underworld? The teeth
of her center already mid-bite[2]. I am a child of Te Waipounamu[3],
the sister without a canoe. The people who call this flying
are lying. There is no joy in a machine bird penetrating a cloud.
I have wanted a painless death. It makes sense. In some species,
the mother swallows her children whole. The word *mother*,
in English, can be used so loosely. It means, a vehicle, an arrival,
a gate forced open; an island; one day, a cluster of islands.

---

1   Rūaumoko is the god of earthquakes, volcanoes and seasons. He pulls on the
ropes that control the land causing the shimmering effect of hot air, called haka of
Tane-rore. He is the husband and uncle of Hine-nui-te-pō, the goddess of death
2   Hine-nui-te-pō waited for death to be brought into the world. Māui
attempted to make mankind immortal by trying to crawl through the goddess' body,
entering in her vagina and leaving by her mouth while she slept, to reverse the path of
birth. Hine woke up; to punish the demi-god, she crushed him with the obsidian teeth
in her vagina. Māui was the first man to die
3   Te Waipounamu is the Māori name for the South Island, meaning the
Water(s) of Greenstone

MYTH #3

Then, there was the middle: our thawed spring,
a noon sun, a treacherous apple core.
I was young enough to love you & old enough
to know it was special.

Together we tight-roped the equator. You
built me a hemisphere. I became a mountain.
You thought I was a volcano. You waited for me
to burst the bubble of your world

with my overflowing kindness. It may still
happen. I could be that girl, but it doesn't matter.
There is no center of the universe.
We exist everywhere.

We are spinning in a bottle. Give me your open
mouth. Suck the rot from my heart.
Be my voyager. Live with me.

LIFE LESSON

I wanted to die & I didn't. My little heart
kept kicking. I kicked down the door
of my mother. I was just a baby
& the whole world happened to me.
      Let me live in the country of its joy.
The continent of my loss has pushed me
out to sea. I could have been a mermaid
but I wanted so badly to be real. I would
be real, but it hurts. This life is teaching me
something I didn't want to learn.
      Let me live in the dream of tomorrow.
I am digging my spirit out from the past
as if I could be worth something. What if
I'm worth something?

CRUSHED

I love men: their hands, the skin around
their nails, how they crack their knuckles
into me; when they make me coffee;
how easily they can walk into the night

& how they never let me walk into the night.

Men who make me flinch-quiet-apologize,
I love their earthquake laughter:
when they tell me I'm funny.

I'm a funny girl, giggling into her own punchline.

Men who hurt me, leave me, lose me,
ask me: *how could you love me when*
you didn't know me?

Oh boy. How else?

LAYERS

Spring, like an old boyfriend, is giving up. I resent
my red dress that I never wear. My legs don't know what
they're for. Here, mid-pilgrimage, are the bravest geese.
Here, mid-city, is the river rippling. I walk for the men

who left. Up ahead is the door to love but I'm tired of
pushing / pulling / propping it open. Let love be.

To the left is the hill I want to climb and never climbed.
I regret the burden of my winter coat. My arms don't
know what they're for. Here, at the top, is the life
I'm peeling away.

BLAME IT ON THE DOG

Can't take a cab ride home
without thinking of someone's fingers on my pulse point.
Ate an orange the other day and remembered his front teeth.

This is not a poem. This is a ghost story.

My father is coming back home, if only in the dog we adopt
and return, adopt and return.

When I apply my lipstick, he whines at my feet.
When I drink water, he nods.

There is a god I am afraid of meeting, but I've been as good
as anyone else.

Today I have an armful of bracelets.
The last time I jingled this much, I loved someone
I should not have loved.

What I am seeing now is scary the way my reflection is scary.

On the train home, I am the blank-eyed woman.
At the daycare center, I am the young girl.

When I hold a baby, I have to remember I was a baby.

The dog cries when he is left alone for too long. Barks until
someone answers.

I started staying home alone when I was eight,
kept my keys at my neighbor's, so no one would ever know.

You are right here, I tell him. *You are okay.*

This apartment is haunted. I've seen three ghosts here,

but maybe that's just us. If you work hard enough,
it's like you're dying.

The faucet is dripping. There is a knock on the door.
My mother snores and my brother sleepwalks to the fridge.
The phone is ringing. Someone wants a small truth.

I am the one crying. I am the one crying.

MIGRATION, PILGRIMAGE,
AND OTHER REASONS TO LEAVE

From my bedroom window, I see a seagull flying
and I am still in bed. The sky is full of his softness,
the world is absent of me.

My best friend tells me she misses me
with such overwhelming sincerity,
I hardly believe her.

The way I love people isn't the way
I want people to love me, all leaving
and coming back and leaving and coming
back and my empty suitcase resting
in someone else's closet.

I'm not like the others, I eat with my hands,
ripped chicken and petals of lettuce, the touch of things.
There is nothing for me here that I can't find
somewhere else:

a man I love,
the man I also love.
I call always urgently,
watch seagulls from my bedroom or his.

How do the birds know when it is going to rain?
Why is it only the people are surprised?

DIRGE

Across the world, people are dying.
Across the country, across the street.
Someone my age. Someone with
my mother's name, my father's face.
Everyday there are more people
asking what to do with the dead,
their bodies, yes, but also their things.
Where do we put their old clothes,
books, awful CD collections? Museums
don't want that garbage. But we can't
just throw it away. What about the hole
in the ozone layer? What about the fish
in the sea? Everything is wrong and there
are people you will never get to meet.
You could have loved them. You could
have borrowed all their favorite things.

DECRESCENDO

My protruding shoulder blades could've been wings,
but they aren't. All childhood I waited for magic. The moon
forgot. So I'm giving up my suspicions of fantasy. No more
about that dying Scorpio sun or the dog ditch that revived him.
I used to be a nymph. I used to dance with the flowers. I used to
sing into the wind & it sounded like the whole world was in love
with me. I was good until I wasn't. One day I sparked into hellfire /
tumbled down the rabbit hole / ripped open the sky.

What rhymes with fasten? Nothing that fits in my forever song.
So I didn't stitch it back together, didn't replace that pulled-down
sun. Anyway, I could never look the sun in the face. I'm not bowing
to a star. Life is a delicacy & I'm starving. Life is a delicacy &
I'm hosting. Come, eat the fruit of my misdemeanor. I'll beg for
forgiveness when it's time to beg. Will you show me how to use
my hands? I have my father's imperfect hands. I can't let it go.
I wish I had wings.

PASSING

What I am most afraid of has happened.
I love my brain, that idiot.

> *(Take care of your favorite memory.*
> *It's wearing away like nail polish on your toes.)*

My toes are so far away from the rest of me.
Sometimes I meet my old body again
in the shower. Why can't she stay?

There's a nightmare unraveling.
Everything I never wanted to lose
has blinked back at me.

Down by the old synagogue,
that was a perfect place.
I loved until I died.
                    (Wait—

NOTES AND ACKNOWLEDGMENTS

Gratitude to the following journals and presses for publishing versions of poems appearing in this book:

Central Avenue Publishing: "THINGS THAT AREN'T TRUE"
Lassi with Lavina: "DIRGE"
The Phoenix: "damsel; WOMAN"
The Rising Phoenix Review: "THE RETELLING"
Where Are You Press: "MIGRATION, PILGRIMAGE, AND OTHER REASONS TO LEAVE"

"A GOOD PLACE" and "THE SECOND MOUNTAIN" are about Camp Rising Sun in Clinton, NY, operated by the Louis August Jonas Foundation, and Camp Rising Sun in Stendis, Denmark, operated by the George E. Jonas Foundation.

"ALTERNATE METHODS OF DATING" is after Lyd Havens.

"DOPPELGÄNGER" references the Bollywood film *Kuch Kuch Hota Hai* (trans. *Something Happens*), directed by Karan Johar in 1998. It is one of the most popular and iconic movies in the Hindi film canon.

"RED CARDINAL" is about and for Tanner Hammond.

"SHLOKA IN BIRDSONG" references the metaphor of the jiva-atman tree that appears in Vedic scriptures, including The Rig Veda samhita (1.164.20-22), Mundaka Upanishad (3.1.1-2), and Svetasvatara Upanishad (4.6-7). This poem also references the incident of the Krauncha birds from the Bala Kanda of Valmiki's version of the Ramayana.

"THE RETELLING" references the Disney film, *The Hunchback of Notre Dame*, directed by Gary Trousdale and Kirk Wise in 1996. This poem also references the Hindu epic, The Ramayana, specifically the version recited by the poet Valmiki.

"THE SECOND MOUNTAIN" references the song "The Climb," recorded by Miley Cyrus for Hannah Montana: The Movie in 2009.

"VIRAHA (विरह) " is for Steven Hopkins.

GRATITUDES

Because I wrote the bulk of this book during the first year of the pandemic, a time that was marked with crushing isolation and grief, VIRAHA is first and foremost a testament to the power, courage, and kindness of the many people who have helped me carry on. Most of these people are nameless to me: my neighbors in Somerville, Allston, and Cambridge; retail workers; baristas; the entire dental staff at Cambridge Health Alliance; the woman who saw me crying on the street and didn't say anything; the woman who saw me crying and smiled. I noticed you too, and I'm grateful you were there.

I am so proud and honored that this book found a home at Game Over Books. Thank you to the entire GOB staff for bringing this text to life: Josh Savory, MJ Malpiedi, Catherine Weiss, Kaleigh O'Keefe, Dena Igusti, Story Boyle, Ally Ang, and Liv Mammone. I am eternally grateful for all the care and attention you've given my work, and the work of my abundantly talented pressmates.

Thank you to Sam Cush for designing the most stunning book cover I've ever seen. You gave my book a face.

I am grateful to my teachers and professors across the globe, from Swarthmore College to Harvard University to the University of Auckland, for helping me cultivate a greater appreciation for mythology and literature. Thank you, especially to Nathalie Anderson, Frank Xavier Clooney, Anand Venkatkrishnan, Nell Hawley, and Smriti Khanal. Thank you to Steven Hopkins, for your guidance, wisdom, and friendship. You were the one who taught me what "viraha" meant. You changed my life.

Thank you to the brilliant, generous, fearless writers who have made the lonely craft of writing lighter and better. Thank you to Amanda Oliver, Fortesa Latifi, Lyd Havens, Lora Mathis, Max Lin, Lyndsay Hall, Victor Pope, Thiahera Nurse, Noel Quiñones, Trista Mateer, Caitlin Conlon, Ari B. Cofer, Clementine von Radics, Kristina Haynes, Gaia Rajan, I.S. Jones, Natalie Wee, and Nikita Gill.

I am so lucky to have such warm, magnanimous friends who remind me with each phone call, visit, TikTok exchange, that I am seen and that the way I understand the world is worth sharing. Thank you to Vivian Chen, Yuan Qu, Liz Kussman, Epiphany Nation, Michael Sheldon, and Janelle Viera for bringing so much joy into my life.

Thank you to my loving, funny, perfect family. Thank you to my brother, Amit Sharma Purmasir, who is the only person on this planet who can make me feel like a kid again. Thank you to Cory, who is the best boy in the whole world. Thank you to my late father, Vivek Sharma Purmasir, for teaching me how to use a computer and how to tell a story and how to keep fighting. Thank you to my mother, Meena Kashyap Purmasir, for giving me the space and tremendous encouragement to write. You fostered in me a deep appreciation for the arts, but more than that you raised me to be brave and creative with my life.

Thank you to Tanner Hammond, my closest friend, roommate, and found family. You were the first person I texted when I found out this book would be published. Apparently, after you checked your phone, you looked up and saw a red cardinal in a tree. And even though you hate superstitions and omens, you told me that it felt like a sign of something good. The funny thing is, you are that sign for me.

Finally, thank you, dear reader. You are the future I have been working towards. I am so grateful that you found me.

BIOGRAPHY

Yena Sharma Purmasir is a poet and essayist from New York City. She was the Queens Teen Poet Laureate from 2010-2011. She is the author of *Until I Learned What It Meant* (Where Are You Press, 2013) and When I'm Not There (self-published, 2016), as well as co-author of *[Dis]Connected Volume 1: Poems & Stories of Connection and Otherwise* (Central Avenue Publishing, 2018). In 2022, she released two new books of poetry: *Our Synonyms: An Epic* from Party Trick Press and *VIRAHA* from Game Over Books. Purmasir holds a master's degree in theological studies from Harvard Divinity School, where she focused on South Asian religious traditions. Currently, she works as a Copy Editor at AppSumo. She resides in Cambridge, Massachusetts and loves the Charles River.